TAO OF HEAVEN, TAO OF EARTH, TAO OF MAN

Tao of Heaven, Tao of Earth, Tao of Man

Secrets of Ancient Shadowboxing

keven-san

WRITERS CLUB PRESS

San Jose New York Lincoln Shanghai

Tao of Heaven, Tao of Earth, Tao of Man
Secrets of Ancient Shadowboxing

Writers Club Press
an imprint of iUniverse.com, Inc.

For information address:
iUniverse.com, Inc.
5220 S 16th, Ste. 200
Lincoln, NE 68512
www.iuniverse.com

ISBN: 0-595-19573-3

Printed in the United States of America

"Substance is the condensation of energy. Functions are many
and varied but they all serve nature."

LAO TZU

Contents

Foreword

In the Autumn of 1995 Sifu keven-san was invited to teach two seminars in Oriental Medicine at Higher Knead Massage School in Albuquerque, New Mexico. The school administration had promised to include a course in this subject, but had failed to do so. The student body was skeptical about the effectiveness of the proposed seminar, fearing that it would not offer us sufficient instruction to meet the requirements of the national Massage Examination.

When we entered the lecture room, however, an interesting array of ancient and modern Chinese philosophical and medical drawing and diagrams immediately piqued our interest. When Sifu keven-san began to teach, we were drawn into a story which began with the ancient Chinese view of the creation of the universe and culminated with practical martial arts applications of some of the healing principals of Chinese Medicine.

Frankly, these seminars represented some of the best instruction we were exposed to during our eight months of study. The combination of intellectual information and practical examples helped us to understand and remember some of the basic principals of Yin/Yang and meridian energy theory. Moreover, Sifu keven-san left us with a few simple acupressure techniques which we could use both personally and professionally.

Although each eight-hour session was held on the weekend, following a full week of classes, both student and faculty remained after the formal instruction was over to ask questions and to compliment Sifu keven-san on his teaching. Our only regret was that his instruction was scheduled at the end of the school year and there was no opportunity to schedule more instruction time with him.

Personally, Sifu keven-san has had a great impact on my practice. For the past two years I have also studied Yang style Tai Chi Chuan with him in our local parks. During these sessions he related the concepts of ancient Chinese philosophy to the martial art. As a result, I have incorporated Chinese music therapy and some acupressure into my massage practice.

I believe Sifu keven-san has a gift for relating these otherwise distant concepts to an American audience. Yet. At the same time, he manages to retain the beauty and ambiance of the ancient teachings.

Lorna Quintero Waddell-Kremer, M.S. Ed., L. M. T.

Preface

Tai Chi Chuan is an Ancient Chinese martial art. Its emphasis is on cultivating suppleness of the body and tranquility of the mind.

The entire theory and practice of Tai Ch Chuan is based on the concept of the Thirteen Forms. Each Form however, represents a function as opposed to a specific technique.

It has been handed down from ancient times that both the substance and function of the Thirteen Forms must be clearly discriminated, if one is the master the art of Tai Chi Chuan.

Introduction

You may work for many years to achieve comfort and social status only to be left with a sense of emptiness and unhappiness. Shadowboxing is a method of transcending this condition by observing, emulating, and celebrating the ways of nature. Logic and analytic thought are not enough to guide you through the process of spiritual unfoldment; you must also develop your instincts and cultivate your sense of intuition. Like the ancient Chinese poem, which follows, the purpose of the "Tao of Heaven" is to pass on to others this far-reaching and un-faded wisdom.

High and low, wise and simple, all busily hoard up the moments of life. How greatly they err! Therefore I have to the uttermost exposed the bitterness both of Substance and Shadow, and have made Spirit show how, by following Nature, we may dissolve this bitterness.

Substance speaks to Shadow:

Heaven and Earth exist forever:
Mountains and rivers never change.
But herbs and trees in perpetual rotation
Are renovated and withered by the dews and frosts;
And Man the wise, Man the divine-
Shall he alone escape this law?
Fortuitously appearing for a moment in the world
He suddenly departs, never to return.
Who will notice there is one person less?
His friends and relations will not give him a thought.
Only when they chance on the things he used
Day in day out, do their spirits sink for a while.
Me no magical arts can save;
Of that I am certain and cannot ever doubt.
I beg you listen to this advice-

When you get wine be sure to drink it.

Shadow replies:

There is no way to preserve life;
Drugs of Immortality are instruments of folly.
I would gladly wander in paradise.
But it is far away and there is no road.
Since the day that I was joined to you
We have shared all our joys and pains.
While you rested in the shade, I left you awhile;
But till the end we shall be together.
Our joint existence is impermanent
Sadly together we shall slip away.
That when the body decays Fame should also go
Is a thought unendurable, burning the heart.
Let us strive and labor while yet we may
To do some deed that men will praise.
Wine may in truth dispel our sorrow,

But how compare it with lasting Fame?

Spirit Expounds

The Tao can only set in motion;
It cannot control the things that it has made.
Man, the second of the Three Orders,
Owes his precedence to Me.
Though I am different from you,
We were born involved in one another;
Nor by any means can we escape
The intimate sharing of good and ill.
The Three emperors were saintly men,
Yet today-where are they?

Peng lived to a great age,
Yet he went at last, when he longed to stay.
And late or soon, all go;
Wise and simple have no reprieve.
Wine may bring forgetfulness,
But does it not hasten old age?
If you set your heart on noble deeds,
How do you know that any will praise you?
By all this thinking you do Me injury;
You had better go where Fate leads
Drift on the Stream of Infinite Flux,
Without joy, without fear;
When you must go-then go,

And make as little fuss as you can.

T'AO CH'IEN   (A.D. Fourth Century)

PART I
TAO OF HEAVEN

Chapter One

Spiritual Faith

In the beginning, the cosmos was without form or function, nothing had happened and nothing existed. This void gave birth to the One, then Chi the natural energy of the One exploded into the two extremities of Yin Chi and Yang Chi. The interaction of the two extremities created the Great Triad of Heaven, Earth, and Man.

Within all things lie the seed of their opposite. Within the womb of Greater Yang, lies the seed of Lesser Yin. Within the womb of Greater Yin, lies the seed of Lesser Yang. These four forces are harmonized by the fifth law of motion which is known as Tai Chi.

The Five Elements: Air, Fire, Earth, Water, and Metal are the five transformational phases in the development of the cosmos: vibration, friction, movement, liquification and solidification. These five transformational phases are the cyclical changes of all things in the natural world.

The Six Chi: Tai Yang, Shao yang, yang Ming, Tai Yin, Shao Yin, and Chiu Yin forecast the location and direction of the six natural forces of Wind, Cold, Heat, Moisture, Dryness, and Inflammation.

The Seven recipes: Ch'I Fang, Go Fang, Tao Fang, Hsao Fang, Huan Fang, Chi Fang and Chung Fang stimulate as well as quiet the seven emotions of Pleasure, Anger, Worry, Reflection, Sorrow, Fright and Terror.

The Eight Great Manifestations: Heaven, Earth, Water, Fire, Thunder, Lake, Wind and Mountain generate the sixty-four hexagrams and display all possible combinations of Yin and Yang; thus, revealing the truth of nature and the meaning of life.

The Ancient Chinese theory of the cosmos and its laws of physics, constitute logical and critical study of both the source and nature of human knowledge. More than mere colloquialisms and quaint proverbs this study meets all the preconditions of a true science. It is equipped with a clear and unambiguous vocabulary; it is consistent and free from internal contradictions; and it is based on a coherent and consequential body of theory.

ANCIENT CHINESE PHYSICS

The Great Void is the first stage of development in the creation of the cosmos. At this point, all is hazy and without distinction; substance and function do not yet exist. This void is ruled by a single primordial law: the law of change; and so from the void comes a single particle of energy that expanded and fragmented to produce everything there is. Evidence of this primordial simplicity as our original source is burned into the heart of every atom.

Physics is the study of particles, forces, and transformational phases. The mathematical formulas of physics reveal that we live in a world of fragmented symmetries that evolved from a state of perfect symmetry. Perfectly symmetrical space is nothingness. The existence of an object would break the symmetry by creating a sense of where it is and where it is not. Perfectly symmetrical time means that nothing has happened. The existence of an event would break the symmetry by creating a sense of before and after the event, and time would then begin to flow in a specific direction. For nothingness, the only possible change is to create energy and mass to break the perfect symmetry of time and space.

Physicists can trace the evolution of the cosmos back to when only two forces were at work, but they cannot find and equation for when there was only one force at work; because that source of energy and mass is the primordial law of change; and particles, forces and transformational phases do not exist in the void.

The cosmos is expanding. Therefore, it has a boundary. On the other side of that boundary is the void; but the void not only surrounds us it is also within us. If you were to partially fill a balloon with dots on it, and imagine yourself standing on one of the dots, as the balloon were more fully inflated it would appear as if you were at the center of expansion, and indeed you would be. If you then completely deflated the balloon all of the dots would merge into one. Eventually if the contraction of the balloon continued event that dot would return to the void, which is our original source. So, the void can be found not only by looking outward but also by looking inward.

The Great Inception is the second stage of development in the creation of the cosmos. At this point, force becomes separated and clearly distinguishable.

As the single particle of energy arose from absolute emptiness, it too was ruled by the most fundamental law of nature, the law of change, and change for an inert mass of energy takes the form of rapid expansion accompanied by extreme heat and brilliant light. Great amounts of subatomic particles were created in this intense heat, but no mass could be accumulated. Gluons, photons and weak bosons bonded and separated just to bond and separate again. At this time only two forces were at work, gravity and the electro-nuclear force. Then, the brilliant light burned out and darkness descended.

The Great Beginning is the third stage of development in the creation of the cosmos. It is at this time that form first appears.

The dawn of light began anew, when the cosmos had expanded and thinned out enough that photons could fly freely without running into other particles. This allowed electrons to settle into orbit around atomic nuclei. The nucleus of an atom is made up of a positively charged particle called a proton and a neutrally charged particle called a neutron. The outer shell of an atom is orbited by negatively charged particles called electrons. One electron orbiting one proton produces the simplest and most abundant of all of the natural elements, a hydrogen atom. Two electrons orbiting a pair of protons produce a helium atom. The first stars consisted almost entirely of hydrogen and helium atoms.

Every single atom inside your body was once inside a star and may well be again someday. The subatomic particles that make up those atoms go back to the very beginning of time. And, time does have a beginning.

The Great Homogeneity is the final stage of development in the creation of the cosmos. It is now that substance and function become clearly distinguishable.

Greater yang, Lesser Yang, Greater Yin, Lesser Yin, these four forces are what the western science of physics describe as the strong nuclear force, the weak nuclear force, electromagnetism and gravity. The integration of these four forces creates a fifth force making them an individual orb of energy known as Tai Chi. Every atom in the cosmos is an integration of these four forces and therefore a complete Tai Chi. The human body is an integration of these four forces and therefore a complete Tai Chi. The gathering and dispersing of atoms is an integration these four forces and therefore a complete Tai Chi. There is nothing beyond or excluded from Tai Chi.

The Great Triad of Heaven, Earth and Man is a simple and lucid image of the cosmos. From the void came a single particle of energy, smaller than the nucleus of an atom and ruled by a single primordial law, the law of change. From that single particle of energy came expansion and from expansion came a boundary without edges where all things return to the void. Form arises from and returns to formlessness. To accept this requires a rational sense of spiritual faith based on a rational framework of the cosmos.

Spiritual faith is a sense of instinct and intuition deeply rooted in the primal memory of our original source. Just as modern science recognizes the existence of rational fear and irrational fear, there is also rational spiritual faith and irrational spiritual faith. When danger is imminent, a rational sense of fear can save your life: such as having found yourself only a few inches form a coiled rattlesnake while sitting on the ground. An irrational fear can cost you your life: such as the girl who drowned herself in the shower trying to flush out her internal organs because of an irrational fear of germs.

Irrational Spiritual Faith is the acceptance of something as true only because of an authoritarian individual or institution. It is rooted in the exploitation of fear and shame and it demands the submission and complete abdication to images, icons and objects. The most fundamental principle of strategy is to divide and conquer; That is why religious institutions unanimously promote a schism between men and women. This not only divides a population of potential servants in half, but by internalizing the schism each individual is divided, and then more easily subjugated and spiritually exhausted. As human beings we are a part of nature and yet separate from it. This separation creates a sense of isolation and loneliness. To find security people often attempt to conform their will to authoritarian individuals and institutions. The widespread vulnerability to be exploited in this particular manner is known in the field of science as the Human Condition.

Rational Spiritual Faith is love and respect for both the internal and external aspects of your own existence. It is rooted in instinct and intuition and it creates a condition of the mind that is free from fear and shame. A rational sense of spiritual faith cultivates personal empowerment. An irrational sense of spiritual faith demands the total abdication of personal power. Our spiritual needs are not one of divine protection, but rather are three of divine union: the internal union of male and female; the external union of two lovers; and the cosmic union with our original source. The way to achieve these three spiritual unions is through the refinements of personal attributes and the channeling of sexual energy to higher centers within your body.

Your body is an individual constellation of energy that is made up of mostly empty space. The solidity of your body is an illusion created by the electromagnetic forces that hold your atoms together. Every day subatomic particles pass through your body like small fish going through a big net because their electromagnetic force is so small it does not interfere with your own. All of the objects that make up the cosmos are also an illusion created by the electromagnetic forces that hold them together as individual orbs of energy. When two objects collide, what really happened was two electromagnetic forces opposed each other. So, through the function atoms and their particles we are related to all things.

The Ancient Chinese compared this relationship between the world of small particle and the physical world to that of a flower and a mirror. It is through the reflection of the flower that the existence of the mirror can be perceived. In the relationship between the world of small particles and the natural world, however, it cannot be decided which is being reflected and which is the reflection.

According to the scripture of the Tao; transcend the illusion of separateness from the natural world and you will transcend the human Condition. Thus, the meaning of life is to touch the human body and be one with nature.

PART II
TAO OF EARTH

Chapter Two

Medicine of
the Three Peaks

ANCIENT CHINESE MEDICINE

In the beginning the human egg is a cosmic void, all is hazy and without distinction. Then Chi, the natural energy of the egg is fertilized by a single sperm cell.

The fertilized egg cell explodes, fragments and multiplies: one cell into two, then four, eight, sixteen, thirty-two, and sixty-four. The single egg cell continues to fragment and multiply until the process creates a three-layered embryo. The Endoderm is the layer that will form the internal organs and their five transformational phases. The Mesoderm will form the bones, muscle and Ti, or substance. The Ectoderm will form the skin, hair and Yun, or function. Ti, substance and Yun, function form a complete Tai Chi and serve as the two wings that will carry the spirit. As the embryo becomes more human in appearance, simple reflexes occur. Breathing becomes coordinated and purposeful. A fetal pulse can be heard.

Ancient Chinese Medicine is a specific method of observation and thought, organized into a clear and unambiguous language. A science uses language to communicate its fundamental principles, concepts, and applications, but it also breaks down nature into a theory that will fit the language. The Latinized terminology of Western Science has been described as a box and the practice of Western Science as an attempt to fit all of nature into it; what will not fit is not observed. The Ancient Chinese did not remove their language of medicine from their language of daily life and while this is considered very unsophisticated by western scientists, it is a much bigger box.

THREE BURNING SPACES

At fertilization, Chi, the natural energy that lies dormant within the human egg explodes into two extremities of Yin Chi and Yang Chi. This explosion creates a specific flow of energy that will continue throughout the life of your body. When you were born, Chi entered your body in the form of air and then began its flow through your Lung Meridian to your Large Intestine, Stomach, Spleen, Heart, Small Intestine, Bladder, Kidneys, Gate of Life, Three Burning Spaces, Gall Bladder and Liver Meridians. The root source of the meridians is your primary Tantien which is located approximately six inches below your navel. The root end of the meridians is your finger tips and toe tips. In Ancient Chinese anatomical prints, the primary Tantien is often depicted as a cauldron because fire is the chemical process that turns matter into energy. Chi flows through your meridians in a very specific direction and at very specific times. Any deviation in this flow of Chi will create symptoms of pain and sickness. The meridians are imbedded deep in your muscle tissue and your internal organs. They emerge to the surface only at certain locations known as Impulse Points. The flow of Chi can be altered or affected by stimulating your Impulse Points along the appropriate meridian.

There are twelve primary meridians, six are Yin and six are Yang. They are arranged symmetrically throughout your body and they correspond to your twelve organs. Each organ in Ancient Chinese Medicine, however, represents a function circle rather than a single entity. A function circle is a group of hundreds of related physiological functions organized into a workable structure. Using the Five Elements of the cosmos to represent these functions is a practical and logical method for applying the laws of physics to the science of medicine.

The six Yang organs that are linked by the six Yang meridians are the Liver, Heart, Spleen, Lungs, Kidneys and Gate of Life. These organs are associated with the season of winter because their function is to store energy. As a storage circle they make up one half a function circle; each Yang organ has a corresponding Yin organ that makes up the completed function circle. Although the sexual organs of men and women are in fact structurally different and appear to be functionally opposites, the male being productive and the female being receptive, it is the function circle of the Gate of Life that produces the flow of sexual secretions and encompasses all of the sexual functions of both men and women.

The six Yin organs that are linked by the six Yin meridians are the Gall Bladder, Small Intestine, Stomach, Large Intestine, Bladder, and Three Burning Spaces. These organs are passage circles and like summer their function is to transform energy. The function circle of the Three Burning Spaces circulates energy and bodily fluids between the Yin organs and the Yang organs. Like an official of rivers, lakes and streams it provides the control and central direction for the energy of the other circles. If the energy of your Three Burning Spaces is evenly distributed then the functions of the storage circles and passage circles will be in harmony.

FOUR LAWS OF MEDICINE

In Ancient Chinese Medicine each human being is considered an individual constellation of energy and therefore, subject to all of the fundamental laws of physics. Just as the entire cosmos is in a constant state of change, the human body is in a constant state of transformational phases. These cyclical transformations must continue without interruption to maintain good health. All external influences on a function circle may be beneficial but only in the proper amount, when this optimum is exceeded the effects will become harmful.

The Law of the Five Elements: Increased activity in one function circle either by intent or illness will increase the activity of the function circle to which it is directly related.

The Mother and Son Law: A meridian that precedes another meridian in the cycle of Chi throughout the body is called the Mother; the meridian that follows is called the Son. To stimulate the physiological functioning of the Son, you must stimulate its Mother meridian.

The Husband and Wife Law: There are three sets of pulses that can be felt on each wrist. The pulse on the left wrist is the Husband and the pulse on the right wrist is the Wife. In a healthy body the Husband pulse is the strongest, for both men and women.

The Noon to Midnight Law: Meridians are more responsive to treatment during specific time of day in accordance with the cycle of Chi throughout your body. These specific times of day can be determined with a special chart used by the ancient Chinese referred to as the Noon to Midnight Clock.

FIVE METHODS OF DIAGNOSIS

A spiritual understanding of health and how to achieve it is more important than the study of disease and how to defeat it. When your Chi is flowing freely and without hindrance, your body is in a condition of health and harmony. Stiff joints, sore muscles and feelings of sickness indicate a blocked or excessive flow of Chi. To make a diagnosis you must first determine the location, direction and cause of the blockage or excessive flow. This kind of diagnosis can only be done by cultivating an internal body awareness of your bones, joints, ligaments, tendons, nerve ganglia, muscles, glands, and organs.

LOOKING

The condition at the surface of your body is a reflection of the condition of your internal organs and systems. There are many sophisticated methods of diagnosis based on looking at and analyzing various parts of the body including the face, tongue, skin color and texture, hands, feet and even body hair. There are also some fundamental principles and concepts that you can apply without being a trained medical professional. The most important element to consider first is the fundamental structure of your body. Skeletal distortions and tight muscles compress the natural pathways of the flow of body fluids and nerve impulses, therefore constricting the flow of Chi to your internal organs and systems. Also, when your muscles tighten and your joints become stiff, your heart is continually stimulated and your adrenal glands keep your body constantly overcharged, exhausted, and more vulnerable to sickness. The skeletal and muscular structure of your body also plays an important part in creating your character and identity. Just as your body can be used to express your thoughts and feelings, it can also be used to suppress them. Observe your body: is your spine twisted, crooked or compressed? Does your head seem to be falling forward or leaning to one side? Do your vertebrae noticeably jut out or sink in? Are your shoulders drawn up or uneven? Are your hands and feet contracted or contorted?

QUESTIONING

Asking your body for its own complaints, explanations, and opinions is an internal technique that must be done in the spirit of relaxation and gentleness. By quieting your mind, calming your senses, and focusing your awareness toward your internal organs and systems, you can evaluate the blockage or excessive flow of Chi caused by skeletal distortions, muscular tension, and the effects of overexposure to the six natural forces. Making a diagnosis in this manner is the art of allowing your body to express its own wants and needs.

LISTENING

The sound of your voice also offers diagnostic signs and signals. You already know what your voice sounds like when your feeling fine and when you are stuffed up or have a sore throat, or even when you are excited or depressed. If you are feeling sick and are quick to become angry and shout this indicates a pathological condition of the function circle of the Liver and Gall Bladder. If you feel as if you are talking incessantly and without pause or purpose this indicates a pathological condition of the function circle of the Heart and Small Intestine. A singsong quality to your voice indicates a pathological condition of the function circle of the Spleen and Stomach. A tendency to cry indicates a pathological condition of the function circle of the Lungs and Colon. Groaning, yawning and snoring all indicate a pathological condition of the function circle of the Kidneys and Bladder.

SMELLING

Everything that you drink and eat affects the odor of your sweat, breath, and waste. The quality of the odor is directly related to the condition of your function circles. Certain odors reflect the condition of certain function circles. This is true whether you are feeling sick or not. A "Rancid" odor of your sweat, breath, and waste indicates a pathological condition of your Liver and Gall Bladder function circles. An odor that could be described as "Scorched" indicates a pathological condition of the function circle of your Heart and Small intestine. A "Fragrant" odor represents a condition of health and harmony for the function circles of your Spleen and Stomach; anything other than a natural and pleasant odor indicates a pathological condition. The odor of something "Rotten" indicates a pathological condition of the function circle of your Lungs and Colon. A "Putrid" odor indicates a pathological condition of the function circle of your Kidneys and Bladder.

TOUCHING

Temperature/Moisture: A high temperature and dryness of your hands and feet indicate a Yang condition. A low or slightly high temperature accompanied by wet hands and feet indicate a Yin condition.

Impulse Points: Locate one of your impulse points and press lightly with the tip of your index finger or the fleshy ball of your thumb, if pain is felt it indicates a Yin condition of the function circle corresponding to the meridian that the impulse point is located on. If no pain is felt, apply heavier pressure, if this heavier pressure induces pain then a Yang condition is indicated. If no pain is felt at all then the corresponding function circle is in good health.

Twelve Pulses: The Ancient Chinese knew that the pulse is dependent on the flow of blood, the flow of blood is dependent on the flow of Chi, and the flow of Chi is dependent on the condition of the function circles. Even modern physicians agree that sickness and disease takes hold in your internal organs and systems before becoming apparent in your body.

The condition of the twelve function circles can be sensed through the twelve pulses. A healthy function circle will reflect a pulse with certain qualities and characteristics. When these differ from what is normal, a pathological excitation or functional inhibition is indicated. A functional inhibition is a blocked flow of Chi. A pathological excitation is an excessive flow of Chi. The twelve pulses mirror even the slightest degeneration in a function circle. Every illness shows up in the pulses before it causes overt symptoms. Pulse diagnosis can reveal symptoms weeks, months, and years in advance other methods.

Before taking your pulse you should lie down or sit quietly for at least ten minutes. Your pulse actually beats very subtly in your own finger tips. Therefore, their effects on what you are sensing must be considered. A man should begin by taking the pulse on his Yang wrist (left) first. A woman should begin by taking the pulse on her Yin wrist (right) first. However, the pulses on both wrists must eventually be considered.

There are three pulse taking points on each wrist, they are called: Tsuan, Chih and Kuan. All three pulse points are felt at the same time and they are all located on the radial artery. Each of the three pulse taking points reflects a separate meridian at two different depths, representing six pulses on each wrist.

To sense your pulse take one of your wrists and bend it back slightly. Place the tips of your first three fingers of your other hand along the radial artery approximately one half inch apart. The first depth is shallow, it is external Yang and it only requires gentle pressure to reach it. The second depth is deep it is internal Yin and requires a much heavier pressure to reach. A respiratory cycle is one inhalation and one exhalation combined. All twelve pulses should beat four times in one respiratory cycle. They should flow freely and without hesitation, but they should also persist with a certain amount of tension. Your pulse is slow when it beats three times or less and fast when it beats six or more times in one respiratory cycle.

Since your body responds to changes in nature so will your pulses.

In Spring, your pulses should be slow, gentle and feel like the strings of a lute.

In Summer, your pulses should be stronger but they will fade away quietly and sound like a sickle cutting through tall grass or a hammer, sharp when they hit and eerily silent as they leave.

In Autumn your pulses should beat lightly and wane quickly till Winter when they will be deep and urgent. Pulses that do not act, as they should according to the seasons indicate a pathological condition of the function circles.

SIX CHI

Symptoms change as an illness progresses or diminishes. Accordingly treatment must correspond not only to the stage that the condition is in, but also the stage that it is headed toward. An illness may go through three Yang and three Yin stages. You have more strength to resist during the first three Yang stages. As your body becomes weakened the illness will progress into the three Yin stages. Death occurs at the extreme point of the final Yin stage of an illness.

Tai Yang: The sickness has not yet penetrated your body's defenses; it is still in your skin and muscles.

Shao Yang: The sickness is half inside your body and half outside; therefore, the symptoms are alternatingly cold and hot.

Yang Ming: The sickness has entered into the meridians of your Stomach and Intestine.

Tai Yin: The sickness has affected the function circle of your Spleen and your stomach cannot transform food and water.

Shao Yin: The sickness has entered the function circle of your Heart and Kidneys.

Chueh Yin: The sickness has damaged all of your organs. There is heat in your upper burner and cold in your lower burner. The Yin Chi has affected the function circle of your Heart and Liver. Death may soon follow.

When the six natural forces of Wind, Cold, Heat, Dampness, Dryness, and Fire, grow extreme or occur out of season they become the cause of sickness and are known as the Six Evils. The Six Evils are associated with extremes of weather and un-seasonal conditions such as intense heat spells, excessive humidity, sudden cold, and high winds.

Wind is the energy of Spring when it usually comes as a mild refreshing breeze. However, summer has its hot winds, autumn has its dry winds, and winter has it cold winds, all of which can blow open the gates of sickness. Symptoms of Wind injury include fevers, chills, profuse sweating, sinus congestion and coughing.

Cold is the energy of Winter and is associated with water. Internal cold arises from a deficiency of Yang Chi within your internal organs; it can cause cold hands, feet, and loss of sexual energy. Symptoms of Cold injury include cessation of sweating and bodily pain.

Heat is the energy of Summer. It can combine with other natural forces to create Damp Heat, Dry Heat, or Wind Heat. Symptoms of Heat injury include headaches, chronic thirst, hot spells, and irritability.

Dampness is the energy of Late Summer, when it usually comes as morning mist, damp ground, humid weather and summer rains. Your internal organs and systems are most vulnerable to Damp injury during sleep. Symptoms include fatigue, cold sweats, and rheumatic pains.

Dryness is the energy of Autumn, it is particularly injurious to the function circle of your Lungs and it combines with other natural forces to create Dry Cold, Dry Heat, and Dry Wind. Internal Dryness arises from insufficient body fluids. Symptoms of Dry injury include constant thirst, dry throat, chapped lips, dry skin, and nausea.

Fire is the energy that causes permanent damage such as cirrhosis of the liver and lung cancer. This type of injury results from prolonged exposure to extremes of any one or more of the other five seasonal energies.

SEVEN RECIPES

Medicinal Herbs are divided into four types of ingredients. Prescriptions are compounded according to a set of ancient rules called the Doctrine of the Seven Recipes. The Emperor is the herbal ingredient that will be the primary curative. The Minister is an ingredient that will act as an aid to the primary curative. The Chancellor is a corrective ingredient that sets the healing process in motion and the ingredient that is used as a vehicle for the prescription is called the Ambassador. Most prescriptions contain all four types of ingredients in varying proportions. The Doctrine of the Seven Recipes helps you decide what the proportion of each should be, according to how far the sickness has progressed.

Ch'I Fang is the Odd Numbered Recipe. When a Yin condition is indicated a prescription may contain an odd number of ingredients such as two Emperor herbs and three Minister herbs to strengthen the Yang.

Go Fang is the Even Numbered Recipe. When a Yang condition is indicated an even number of Emperor and Minister herbs are used to strengthen the Yin.

Ta Fang is the Great Recipe. These prescriptions are used in response to very serious conditions which display a complex set of symptoms. These remedies are very powerful and sometimes contain small amounts of poisonous herbs.

Hsao Fang is the Little Recipe. Sometimes only two or three ingredients are needed to treat a simple condition, which displays only one symptom.

Huan Fang is the Slow Recipe. When a physical condition is too weak to absorb more powerful herbs these gentle remedies are used to build strength.

Chi Fang is the Emergency Recipe. The effects of these remedies are immediate and are used in cases of near death to increase the activity of Chi within the body.

Chung Fang is the Repeated Recipe. These prescriptions contain many herbs and are taken repeatedly over the course of a sickness. They are used to treat many organs and systems at the same time.

Each of the five original function circles corresponds to a specific emotion. Three of the five function circles correspond to a single emotion. Two of the five function circles correspond to two separate emotions making seven emotional symptoms in all. Extreme excesses of these emotions will have a degenerative effect on their corresponding function circle.

Pleasure is the emotion of the Heart. It is the great stimulus of your imagination and your reserves of energy. If you become too preoccupied with pleasure, however, it will cause a degenerative condition of the function circle of your heart. Symptoms include confusion, lack of muscular coordination and disorganized behavior.

Anger and frequent displays of violence affect the function circle of your Liver. Symptoms include a bright red face and in extreme cases even cerebral hemorrhage.

Worry and severe anxiety have their most pronounced effects on the function circle of your Lungs. Anxiety has the effect of disrupting the rhythm of all of your vital functions. This may give rise to a number of symptoms including shortness of breath, coughing up large quantities of phlegm, and loss of appetite followed by a general loss of muscle tone.

Reflection can lead to forgetfulness and debilitation when it becomes excessive, at which time it will have a degenerative effect on the function circle of your Spleen and thus on the underlying rhythm of all the function circles. Symptoms may include night sweats and serious weight loss to the point of malnutrition.

Sorrow is an adjutant to the primary emotion of Worry; it depletes the energy of the function circle of your Lungs. Therefore, in accordance with the principles of the five transformational phases it also depletes the energy of your Heart. A pale and haggard face is the only symptom of this condition.

Fear is likely to have a deleterious effect on the function circle of your Kidneys. This is true whether it is a powerful sudden fright or the kind of dull nameless fear that so many men and women carry around with them and has become characteristic of our society. Symptoms include indecision, restlessness, depression, and paranoia.

Terror drastically depletes the energy of the function circle of your Heart. Symptoms include rapid breathing and incoherent speech.

EIGHT METHODS OF THERAPY

Breath, Blood, Bone Marrow, Semen, and the Ovum are all different physical manifestations of the same metaphysical energy, Chi. Since heat rises upward, stimulating sexual energy is like stoking the fire beneath the cauldron of your primary Tantien. This in turn, fans the flames of your internal organs and systems thereby burning up the impure energies that have collected in various parts of your body. Just as your brain and nervous system affect your behavior, your behavior affects your brain and nervous system.

Measured strokes of sexual intercourse have a direct effect on your respiration, heartbeat, circulation, glandular secretions and brain waves. This allows your body to create antidotes for any condition by triggering the correct metabolic processes. Specific postures channel energy in different ways enabling your body to focus on and correct subtle imbalances of Yin Chi and Yang Chi. You should not attempt to count the strokes out loud or even use verbal language without moving your lips, rather, you should measure the strokes against a naturally occurring rhythm or the rhythm of background music.

The eight methods of therapeutic sex should be practiced without any emission of semen. While the man perfects his powers of retention, the woman must perfect her powers of receiving and circulating the healing energies of her spirit. If a woman truly opens up her awesome powers of rejuvenation there is no limit to her healing potential.

To concentrate semen the woman should lie on her side with her legs spread wide open, the man should then lie between her legs, insert his Jade Stalk and give her eighteen strokes of love. This method not only concentrates the semen it also cures any bleeding of the woman. It should be performed twice a day for fifteen days.

To rest the spirit the woman should lie on her back with her legs stretched out and her butt raised on a cushion. The man should then kneel between her open legs, insert his Jade Stalk, and give her twenty-seven strokes of love. This method not only rest the spirit of the man it will also cure any chills in the sexual region of the woman. It should be performed three times a day for fifteen days.

To benefit the internal organs the woman should lie on her side and lift both of her knees to her breast. The man should then lay his body at a right angle across her, insert his Jade Stalk from behind and then give her thirty-six strokes of love. This method not only benefits the internal organs of the man but also of the woman. It should be performed four times a day for twenty days.

To strengthen the bones the woman should lie on her side with her left leg raised and her right leg stretched out. The man should then lay on top of her, rest his weight on his arms, insert his Jade Stalk and give her exactly forty-five strokes of love. This method not only harmonizes the joints of the man, it will also cure any congestion in the body of the woman. It should be performed five times a day for a period of ten days. To harmonize the circulation of blood, the woman should lay on her side, bending her right leg and extending her left leg. The man should lie over her, rest his weight on his hands and then allow her to insert his Jade Stalk for exactly fifty-four strokes of love. This method not only promotes the circulation of blood in the man, it is also effective in curing any pains in the sexual region of the woman. It should be performed six times a day for twenty days.

To increase the blood the man should lie on his back and woman should kneel over him, then with her butt still raised he inserts his Jade Stalk deeply. The woman moves up and down for exactly sixty-three strokes of love. This method not only increases a man's blood and builds up his strength; it is also effective in curing any irregularities of the woman's menstruation. It should be performed seven times a day for ten days.

To balance the elements the woman should lie flat on her front, with her face down and butt raised on a cushion. The man should then lay on top of her, insert his Jade Stalk from the rear and give her exactly seventy-two strokes of love. This method not only harmonizes the twelve function circles in both the man and woman, it also increases the production of their bone marrow. It should be performed eight times a day for as long as it takes to produce results.

To adjust the whole physical system the woman should lie on her back with both of her legs folded under her in such a way that her butt rests on her feet. The man should lean over her with his legs apart, insert his Jade Stalk from the rear and give her exactly eighty-one strokes of love. This method not only strengthens the bones and revitalizes the whole being of the man, it also cures any sexual problems of the woman. It should be performed nine times a day for nine days.

MEDICINE OF THE THREE PEAKS

At the end of your childhood your body entered puberty and develop a physical need for the production, circulation and secretion of special body fluids, which contain sexual hormones. The exchange and consumption of these sexual hormones with a lover can be powerful medicine.

The mouth is known as the Red Lotus Peak and the medicine that flows from it is called Heavenly Pool. It emanates from beneath the tongue and is almost transparent in color. When it is produced in abundance you should endeavor to swallow it. This medicine adds fluidity to your internal organs and systems.

The nipples are known as The Double Lotus Peaks and the medicine that flows from them is called White Snow. White Snow is not the breast milk produced by women but rather a secretion spontaneously generated by sexual excitement. When the nipples are sucked the sexual organs contract and this in turn affects glandular secretions. When deeply sucked the medicine of the Double Lotus Peaks can reach as far as the Heavenly Pool above and descend as far as the Mysterious Gate of Life and Death.

The lower peak is known as the Mysterious Gate and the medicine that flows from a man's Mysterious Gate is called the Jade Fluid, drinking the Jade Fluid is the best way to increase one's Yang Chi. The medicine that flows from a woman's Mysterious Gate is call Moon Flower Waters. The doorway to women's Mysterious Gate is usually closed but when it is aroused during love making to such an extent that emanations from the Heart begin to exude outward this inner doorway opens. When a woman reaches the climax of pleasure her moisture flows freely downward. If her moisture is absorbed directly through the mouth it integrates the two poles of the body and creates a healthful exchange of secretion energies. It can also be absorbed by withdrawing the Jade Stalk until it is at the depth of a thumb tip and then creating a negative pressure in the bladder, this will benefit the man's original Yang force and nurture his inner spirit. By opening up the healing energies of her spirit the woman also receives, her Yin force is enhanced and her healing powers are restored

Chapter Three

Tui Shou

Once upon a time in Ancient China, a master of the mystical arts climbed into the Wu Dang mountains and made his home, intending to live out his life there in harmony with nature, believing that the highest good is to do no harm. Then, one night, the Eight Great Immortals visited him in a dream and taught him Tai Chi Chuan, after which he was returned to the world of people so that he could pass on to others what had been passed on to him.

For many years he wandered through the nine provinces carrying only a few possessions. He treaded down frosty roads, crossed jagged mountains, and forded great rivers. The villagers affectionately called him "Sloppy Chang," because he had a weathered face with deep gray eyes that were framed by long white hair and a beard. They said he was a healer who could chase away evil demons and a warrior that could summon the spirit of dragons. They said he defeated a hundred men in a single day with his martial art skills. Eventually the Emperor Ming Tai Tzu sent for him to teach Tai Chi Chuan to his soldiers but "Sloppy Chang" refused to even go to the Imperial Court.

As he continued on his travels the wisdom of his ways spread throughout the land. And, this is what he taught to those he considered worthy:

"The Five Elements are Advance, Retreat, Look Left, Look Right, and Central Equilibrium. The Eight Great Manifestations are Push, Rollback, Ward Off, Press, Elbow Stroke, Split, Pluck and Shoulder Stroke. Thus, the Five Elements and Eight Great Manifestations are the Thirteen Forms of Tai Chi Chuan. If you do not seek carefully in the direction indicated, your efforts will be in vain and you will have cause to sigh with regret."

When he grew old, Sloppy Chang returned to the mountains and built a small hut. Gathering herbs to sell in the village market, he lived the rest of his life in harmony with nature, always believing that the highest good is to do no harm.

TUI SHOU

Tai Chi Chuan is both a martial art and a therapeutic method of movement based on the principles and concepts of Ancient Chinese Medicine.

The Thirteen forms, however, are conceived of as functions rather than specific techniques in the exact same way that each organ is regarded as a function circle rather than a single entity. The very first form or function is Central Equilibrium; it is applied to and performed in conjunction with all other forms. The remaining twelve forms are initially learned in the following sets of two because it is the nature of a function to be directly related to or dependent upon a corresponding action or function.

Central Equilibrium

Advance	Retreat
Look Left	Look Right
Push	Rollback
Ward Off	Press
Elbow Stroke	Split
Pluck	Shoulder Stroke

Tui Shou is often referred to as single-handed push-hands and it is the most fundamental of all Tai Chi Chuan training drills. It must be practiced with both the right and left sides, but in this chapter for the sake simplicity and clarity we will refer to the right hand forward position only.

Both opponents begin from a connected position and stay connected throughout the exercise.

First, they reach out with their right fists and touch knuckles, checking their distance and making sure that their hips and shoulders are perfectly square to each other.

Second, they step out with their right foot so that each foot is toe to heel and approximately one fist width apart. Then they connect wrist to wrist with the backs of their right hands nearly touching.

Third, the opponents attack each other's center of gravity by pushing smoothly and defend themselves by dissolving the other's momentum while maintaining their connected position without interruption.

CENTRAL EQUILIBRIUM

Function: To balance opposing forces along a central axis.
Substance: A steady, even, perfectly clear, mind.

There are two central axis on the human body that you must seek to refine. The first is vertical; along which you must learn to rotate as if it were an axle running through the center of your body. When one shoulder is pushed the other turns like a revolving door.

The second is horizontal, approximately three inches below the navel. It is the line at which your body would fold if you were to bend over while keeping your back straight, and knees locked. The ability to bend and revolve on a dual axis while maintaining a central equilibrium will give your body the dynamics of a weighted punching bag that cannot be pushed over.

Besides cultivating an awareness of your two physical axis you must also cultivate a central equilibrium of your mind. Regular practice of Tai Chi Chuan can relieve your mind of the pathological excitations and functional inhibitions caused by everyday stress; thus achieving a central equilibrium of your psyche.

ADVANCE

Function: To shift the center of gravity, forward.
Substance: To gain advantage, and secure control.

In some martial art styles students are taught to drive off the rear leg when moving forward.

This creates a push-pull method of propulsion that tends to keep the back leg stuck to the ground.

Tai Chi Chuan, however, relies on a weight-shift-pull method of propulsion. This is done by the bending of your front knee as the initiating action, as opposed to pushing with the rear leg.

RETREAT

Function: To shift the center of gravity, backward.
Substance: To withdraw from danger, seek refuge, or seclusion.

The same weight-shift-pull method of propulsion applies to shifting backward. This time your initiating action is the bending of the knee of your rear leg.

LOOK LEFT

Function: To rotate along a vertical axis in order to start, direct, or alter the flow of motion.
Substance: To send, drive, or create a shock.

From the most basic position of right leg forward, it is this form that begins the ebb and flow of push-hands training. This form is also sometimes referred to as "dodge left and beware of right".

LOOK RIGHT

Function: To revolve around a vertical axis in order to stop, reject, or change the course of a linear motion.
Substance: To become transformed and gain the opportunity to counter attack.

Again, from the most basic position of right leg forward. This action allows you to deflect the oncoming advance while maintaining your central equilibrium. This form is also sometimes referred to as "dodge right and beware of left."

PUSH

Function: To move the center of gravity of an object, by exerting force.
Substance: An energetic drive, thrust, or force.

As a martial art, Tai Chi Chuan contains numerous strikes and kicks. All of these are examples of the form "push". It is easy to imagine a bullet as pushing its way through a bale of hay.

While a bullet fired at a board would create a powerful, shattering, impact, it too could be described as pushing its way through the wood. The strikes and kicks of Tai Chi Chuan should be considered similar to a bullet pushing its way through the target at great speed.

ROLLBACK

Function: To wrap in upon self or central axis.
Substance: The reduction of steady or increasing momentum.

This form, or function, is used to lead an opponent's attack further than he intended it to go; therefore leaving him overextended and vulnerable to counterattack.

WARD OFF

Function: To repulse, project, or rebound outward.
Substance: It is the express purpose of this form to guard, protect, or otherwise avert danger.

When performing this technique in push-hands training the arm makes a figure eight movement using either hip vibration or hip rotation.

PRESS

Function: To constrict, constrain, pursue, or force into a particular shape or form.
Substance: To exert force.

The form "press" is the most appropriate response to "ward off" in basic push-hands.

You want to first constrain your opponent's attack and then force his linear motion into a desired course that you can control and from which you can gain advantage.

The difference between Push and Press is that it is the function of Push to forcefully impact on a center of gravity while the function of Press is to redirect energy.

ELBOWSTROKE

Function: Attacking directly and head on, without attempting to dissolve the opponent's power and momentum first.
Substance: It is the combined momentum of two forward moving objects that make this a powerful and effective technique.

This form sounds like a very specific technique and it is in fact performed as an elbow strike in fundamental push-hands training. However, it is also performed as a back-fist strike and other techniques. That is because, it is the essential character or essence of this form to alternate substantial and insubstantial between the elbow and fist.

SPLIT

Function: To divide, break, or separate parts of a single unit into opposing factions.
Substance: Spinning or spiraling your opponent outward.

In basic push-hands training the form split is used to defend against the form elbow-stroke by pushing upward on the attackers elbow and downward on his wrist. You must maintain control of the wrist to prevent counterattack.

PLUCK

Function: To stretch, break, or tear from a fixed position by boosting momentum long a course or path that it is already on.
Substance: A complete coordination of timing, distance, and force.

This is perhaps the most difficult of all of the forms to learn, because it requires you to pick up on and control the opponent's timing and force much earlier than other techniques.

SHOULDERSTROKE

Function: To shift intent from your fist to your shoulder and back.
Substance: Turning sudden loss into a single continuous movement from which you can regain control.

In basic push-hands when you are pulled off balance this technique is applied by stepping forward and then dropping the entire weight of your body onto the opponent with your shoulder, his grasp of your wrist then becomes insubstantial; allowing you to regain control. You must make no attempt to break your own fall; simply control the direction of the fall and invest into loss.

All of the Forms described in this section can be applied in an infinite variety of actual techniques. Practicing them in this paticular order of progress first allows beginners to learn each of the Thirteen Forms in their most simple and direct manner.

THE MOUNTAIN AND THE RIVER

As a beginner, Tui Shou requires conscious thought and effort because you are learning basic hand and foot movements. Eventually, your body will develop the ability to listen through your wrist. Then your unconscious mind can monitor your opponent's intent and decipher his weaknesses. By allowing your conscious mind to be engaged in conversation or thought, you can actually assist your unconscious mind to control your movements naturally and without hindrance; because your unconscious mind has no fear or desire.

When your mind is excited or upset, the natural functions of your body also tend to be disturbed. When your mind is free from fear and desire, your body can act spontaneously and without any personal awareness or intervention.

Fear comes from going against the current of circumstances; in a fight your movements must flow with that of your opponent. Desire comes from attachment to your ego, if you cherish even one single illusion, separation of intent and technique will come; just as there is separation between the mountain and the river.

Chapter Four

San Shou

There are many forms of push hands training: single handed, double handed, in place, in line, in four directions, sticky hands, pull hands and push feet. All of these training methods have at least one thing in common; two opponents begin from a connected position and stay connected throughout the exercise. While these training methods are effective in developing both skill and understanding in the use of the thirteen forms, eventually you have to practice powerful realistic attacks and defensive maneuvers. This type of training is called San Shou. An analogy often used in teaching San Shou is that of playing catch with a ball and glove; when the ball is thrown rather than bracing for impact, you reach out for it, absorb its momentum gently and then without interruption return it to the sender. This is the essential character and essence of San Shou attracting, connecting, dissolving and discharging.

ESSENCE OF POWER

There are three different levels of San Shou training.

The first level of San Shou training is understanding power. To understand the dynamics of a realistic attack you must experience a realistic attack. This requires a highly skilled partner who has the ability to follow his opponent and punch on target.

The second level of San Shou training is receiving power. To receive power one must learn to invest in loss. This is called inviting the robber in. If you do not invite the robber in then he cannot steal from you but neither can you catch him. To receive power means not only to respond but also to welcome in and then to constrict, constrain, or convert the flow of motion.

The third level of San Shou training is transferring power. Power in martial arts is often described in the following mathematical formula; mass x speed = force. Mass is the weight of your body accumulated at your center of gravity; if you double its speed you quadruple its power. To transfer power from the center of gravity through your body and into a target, you must learn to create energy as if you are drawing a powerful bow and then release the energy as if shooting an arrow.

San Shou is the art of dissolving the momentum of a thousand pounds with the force of a single ounce. All San Shou training drills begin from a disconnected position, opponents typically stand three to five feet apart. Once an attack has been made the defender must "connect" and then redirect the power, as opposed to "blocking" which is more like bracing for impact. The three primary connecting points on the arm are the wrist, elbow, and shoulder. The three primary connecting points on the leg are the ankle, knee and hip. It is important that your San Shou training begin with basic exercises that are designed to develop some skill in "connecting" before advancing into what might be described as true free fighting.

The Whipping Branch is a cross arm connect. Like a branch that has been pulled back and then released, the open hand whips across the body connecting palm to wrist and deflecting the attack. When both hands are used to perform this technique, the first connects palm to wrist and the second connects the edge of the palm to elbow in rapid succession.

The Leaping Deer is same arm connect. The action of this technique is a fast spring like motion similar to a deer that has been startled from its hiding place. Bounding upward the open hand connects palm to wrist in a leaping motion. When performed properly the back of the deflecting hand will be parallel to the ear on the same side of your body and the elbow will be slightly higher than the wrist.

The Swooping Bird is a two arm connect. Your own two arms are connected wrist to wrist and make an X shape. The movement is circular and flowing, the appearance is like that of a hawk seizing a rabbit.

THE FIVE TARGETS

In any way of striking you must do it with intent and resolution. This requires knowledge of the five primary target areas of the human body. The five primary targets are:

The Skeletal system functions as a support structure, a site of attachment for muscles, ligaments, and tendons. It is also a source of calcium and blood cell development for the entire body. The articular system is the joints that connect your bones; they are functionally classified as immovable, partly movable, or freely movable.

The Muscular system acts like a series of pulleys and levers operating a skeletal joint. Muscles are named in relation to their attachment, shape, number of heads, function and position.

The Circulatory system includes the heart which pumps blood into arteries and receives blood from veins, and capillaries which are extremely thin walled vessels throughout the body that permit the exchange of nutrients between the vessels interior and exterior, they in turn receive blood from small arteries and conduct blood to small veins.

The Respiratory system conducts air to the lungs where the blood can readily absorb it; it also removes carbon dioxide-laden air from the lungs and exhausts it to the external atmosphere. The respiratory system consists of the nose, mouth, esophagus, lungs and diaphragm.

The Nervous system regulates involuntary body functions such as breathing and the muscular contractions that move food through your intestines. The nervous system is also responsible for sending messages to the brain that allow for sensory awareness, emotions, rational thought, memory and language.

More often than not an attack will affect several of these system at the same time. To penetrate the body and make your attack affective it is important to make a clear distinction between your primary target and secondary targets. For example, a grappling technique might put equal emphasis on both the muscular system and the skeletal system therefore you must understand which muscles are pulling on which joints and why. An attack to the upper rib cage just under the arm pit would affect the skeletal system, muscular system, and the nervous system, but its primary target is the respiratory system, therefore you must strike with the intent of attacking the respiratory system as opposed to simply attacking the way you might thump the outside of a heavy bag.

T'UI-NA

There are many books videos and charts illustrating the location of nerve strikes and vital target areas for martial artist. These resources also offer numerous techniques for attacking various points on the body. However, students who have tried to learn from such resources typically end up with three unanswered questions. How do you instantly find an impulse point on an opponent? How do you know exactly how hard to strike to be effective? And, what kind of reaction or physiological response can you expect? The answer to all three questions can be found in the practice of Tui Na, which is the art of Ancient Chinese massage.

This ancient art consist of seven fundamental techniques which should be practiced as both self massage and partner massage with an equal emphasis on giving and receiving; experiencing these sensations is the only true way to learn them.

Mo; to manipulate or to drive out energetically and disperse blocked chi.

Ch'ia; to pinch is the action of digging the nail into the skin so that it serves the same purpose as the acupuncturist's needle.

Ju; to rub involves making circular motions around the area being treated.

Tui; is to press which is the action of pushing directly on an impulse point.

Yun; to transport, or set in motion, is to stimulate the circulation of the blood by means of a slow, light, movement.

Tso; is the action of rolling the skin between the hands or between two fingers.

Yao is simply the technique of shaking

ACCUPRESSURE

Most of the techniques of Tui Na are also common to western styles of massage therapy. The art of acupressure, which is unique to the Ancient Chinese and directly related to acupuncture consist of five fundamental techniques, which should be applied to all acupressure treatments.

Probe gently until you locate the center point of a depression or cavity within the muscular and skeletal structure.

Gradually increase pressure until you feel you have reached to bottom of the depression or cavity.

Hold for three to ten seconds or three to ten minutes depending on the treatment plan.

Gradually release the pressure using your internal sense to listen to the movement of the chi.

Palm the area gently allowing the warmth or your hand to facilitate the flow of the chi.

KWAT SU

In the practice of martial arts accidental injuries can be expected therefore, the Ancient Chinese created a method of first aid massage techniques and emergency resuscitation techniques. These techniques however, can do more harm than good where the injury is so severe that it has caused visceral or vascular damage.

In laryngeal trauma; the patient should be seated on the floor and the spinal column should be lightly tapped with the index and middle fingers at the level of the seventh cervical vertebra. The percussion technique should be done using the middle sections of the fingers between the first and second joints.

In epigastric trauma the subject should be laid on his back with arms crossed and legs straight. The epigastric region, which is the area of the solar plexus and upper abdomen, is then pressed vigorously and repeatedly

In testicular trauma; the patient is laid on his back. The instructor then grasps the patient's ankle and pulls his leg toward him fully extending it. He may in addition proceed to counterextend the limb by placing his bare left foot on the subject's abdomen. The fist is then used to pound the middle of the inside of the foot with a single sharp blow and loud shout.

The patient may also lie on his stomach for percussion of the upper part of the ilium above and within Petit's triangle. This is the area of the upper portion of the hip bone and the triangular shape formed by the crease of the leg.

Or, lastly the patient may be placed in a lying position once again and his inguinal canal, which is the area of and near the groin, is lightly tapped along the line of the spermatic cord. The spermatic cord is the structure suspending a testicle within the scrotum and containing the blood vessels and nerves that supply the testicles.

In cerebral trauma; percussion of the third lumbar vertebra and cervical massage are indicated. The patient should be seated on the floor and you should lightly tap the area of the lower back on both sides of the spinal column using the same section of the index and middle fingers as used in cases of laryngeal shock. This should be followed with a general massage of neck and shoulders.

In cases of apparent death the patients clothes should be loosened and the instructor should pinch the skin below the navel then pull and twist until the patient is lifted off of the floor.

Where breathing has stopped Kwat su employs a compression of the patients thorax technique, in which one hand is placed on top of the other and you gently lower your weight onto the patients torso to stimulate inhalation.

When the heart has stopped it may be restarted by placing one hand flat against the chest and thumping it with the other.

SNOW AND THE BAMBOO LEAF

In San Shou what you are trying to achieve is not a higher level of consciousness but a lower one. You are attempting to return to the pure and natural human condition that you have lost through the artificial arrangement of rewards and punishment. This level of consciousness is without desire for gain or profit and is known as letting go of the ego. If your mind is fettered by thoughts of the praise and adoration that comes with success, then those thoughts will, by necessity, also consist of the shame and disapproval that comes with failure. This is called clinging to the ego and it creates a distorted view of life. To transcend the problem of your ego you must learn to respond to a strike with the casual nonchalance of snow falling from a bamboo leaf. The bamboo leaf bends lower and lower under the weight of the snow, then, when the tension is fulfilled, the snow suddenly slips to the ground without the bamboo leaf having stirred. This level of consciousness is one of waiting for fulfillment as opposed to bracing yourself for impact.

Chapter Five

Shadowboxing

Shadowboxing is a training method in which your partner is your own shadow cast on the ground by the sun or on the wall by a candle flame. It is a series of individual postures threaded together in an uninterrupted sequence. This type of solo sequence training is also call longboxing because it rolls on unceasingly like the stream of a large river and softboxing because your muscles are relaxed, your movements are slow, and external force is not applied. When your muscles are relaxed and your mind is clear, Chi will circulate throughout your body.

Postures and rituals help channel your Chi. When you perform a ritual your are not simply seeking the right way to do it according to a set of rules, you are seeking oneness with your primal memory. The cosmos was a void, and then it created a vibration. The vibration generated movement, friction, liquification, and solidification. That primordial vibration still emanates today, from the center of the Earth and all of the celestial orbs in Heaven as well as from the center of your own body. When you tune into the primordial vibration you attain oneness with our original source and this is called spiritual transcendence.

Shadowboxing is also a method of cultivating both the internal and external dynamics of the thirteen forms. The external dynamics are timing, distance, and force. The internal dynamics are intent, Chi, and wisdom. Intent is cultivated by directing the Chi. Chi is cultivated by developing suppleness. Wisdom is cultivated by discriminating the substantial from the insubstantial. "The mind directs the Chi, the Chi directs the body, the body directs the Shadow."

THREE LEVELS & NINE DEGREES

Tai Chi Chuan does not have any formal test or belt rank structure, instead there are three levels and nine degrees of training which are both a set of ancient principles, concepts, and applications; as well as an order of progress.

The Human level first degree is the technique of relaxing the ligaments in your wrists, then your elbows, and finally your shoulders, from softness alone will you progress.

The Human level second degree is the technique of relaxing the ligaments in your ankles, then your knees, and finally your hips. To achieve this you must be able to clearly discriminate the substantial from the insubstantial.

The Human level third degree is the technique of relaxing the ligaments in your spine; your head should feel as if it were suspended by a thread from Heaven.

The Earth level first degree is the technique of sinking the Chi to your primary Tantien, this must happen naturally and cannot be forced.

The Earth level second degree is the technique of directing the Chi from the waist to the Bubbling Spring point on the bottom of your feet and then up to the Lao Kung point in the palm of your hand.

The Earth level third degree is the technique of circulating the Chi evenly throughout the Three Burning Spaces, longevity and good health will be the natural reward.

The Heaven level first degree is the technique of listening to strength; then when you make contact with your opponent's Chi you can anticipate his movements.

The Heaven level second degree is the technique of comprehending internal power, Chi flows through your ligaments, blood vessels, membranes and diaphragm, generating four kinds of internal power: defensive, concealing, readiness, and attacking.

The Heaven level third degree is the level of Spiritual Power, when your Chi reaches its highest point it becomes mental energy and is called the power without physical force; wherever the eyes concentrate, the spirit reaches and the Chi follows.

SHADOWBOOK

A shadowbook is a personalized journal of your own training and development. It is comprised of a pithy of verses in which words and phrases can be expanded into discourses. This is a practical and logical method of managing hundreds of related principles, concepts and applications.

In an educational based structure every lesson is dependent on the previous one and directly related to the next one. Also, every lesson is considered a small step, leading to a short-term goal, for the purpose of achieving a long-range objective.

Art transcends the Human Condition by harmonizing the cosmic vibrations of the artist; the medium, and the audience, crass commercialism compounds the Human Condition by fragmenting, isolating and separating people from the natural world.

In an art based structure every lesson is completely independent of the previous one and unrelated to the next. Also, each lesson serves a purpose as opposed to leading to a goal. An art based structure is like the pith of a flower that leads to the unfoldment of its petals. The purpose of each lesson is simple observation and direct experience. The emphasis of an art based structure is not on how to do Shadowboxing but on how to integrate it into your daily life as a sense of spiritual faith.

The pithy verses contained in the appendiced "Shadowbook" are my own personalized verses and were not designed for a reader without experience to be able to follow. They describe physical exercises which were included for the purposes of inspiration and guidance. Pithy verses are fragmented words and phrases that are chosen for their flow and imagery; not for memorizing and reciting but for reflecting upon and making a "personal artistic interpretation."

Art is not a thing, it is a function and it is the function of art to transcend the Human Condition thus, artistic interpretation is fundamental to an art based structure. Each shadowboxing posture has an artistic name and for the posture to be performed correctly you must make a personal artistic interpretation. The concept of a personal artistic interpretation is based on the principle of "fifty percent effort and fifty percent imagination." This principle can be applied to all facets of life including child rearing, love making, martial arts, business and politics. To not try too hard, to not be too much, to not have too much, these are recurring themes throughout Ancient Chinese art and philosophy. Old men and young boys were assigned to sweep the temple courtyards so there would always be some dirt left in the corners and a few leaves still blowing around. This practice was common because a simple and art based spiritual faith requires a simple and art based life.

PART III

TAO OF MAN

Chapter Six

Spiritual Enlightenment

Spiritual Enlightenment is your own personal emancipation from religious institutions and their distorted reflections of life. The way to dissolve these distorted reflections is through the refinement of personal attributes and by channeling sexual energy to higher centers within your body.

HIGHER CENTERS

The Mysterious Gate of Life and Death is a secondary Tantien located midway between the anus and the genitals. It centers around a point called Hui-Yin and lies amidst the endings of many blood vessels and nerve endings. Rather than being a specific muscle or organ, it is the general region of your genitals and encompasses all sexual functions for both men and women. It is from here that you must first create sexual energy and then direct that energy to other secondary Tantiens within your body. Directly above the Mysterious Gate is either your Sperm Palace or your Ovarian Palace. Both of these regions are a great source of energy. The Sperm Palace is located in the area of the prostrate gland and seminal vesicles just above the Jade Stalk. The Ovarian Palace is located midway between the ovaries and one and one/half inches below the surface of the skin.

From the Palace energy rises up to your primary Tantien, as blood and Chi are drawn to this area a deep rhythmic breathing begins to pump energy throughout your body so that no excess energy can build up and no deficiency can go unfulfilled. The belly button is considered the Root of Life because in the womb a fetus is linked to life through its umbilical cord and after birth it continues to receive its primary source of energy from the same area.

The next level that you must direct the energy to is Shun Chung. This is your heart and it is the center for rejuvenation and love. It is located midway between the nipples and concentrating on this area very quickly leads to ecstasy.

As the energy continues to rise it should be directed to your Shang Tantien. This point is located midway between your eyebrows and is also called the Jade Cauldron. It is the center of vision and memory as well as abstract and conceptual thinking.

Now look into the center of your head and direct the energy to the One Hundred Meeting Point which is located above the mid-brain; when it reaches this far it will become spiritual energy and dissolve all of the distorted reflections of religious institutions and ideologies.

The rise of sexual energy to higher centers within your body is a naturally occurring process; to master the function requires time and effort. Begin, by simply experimenting and observing the results. Then, gain control of the results in small incremental steps by expanding and contracting the Hui Yin and pressing, stroking, or rubbing, the other energy enters in their order of progress. Finally, fine-tune the results into an act of transcendental ecstasy and spiritual worship by performing them with an awareness of your own existence and sense of proper conduct.

The foundation of society is the individual human being, thus, the future of society is dependent upon individual spiritual enlightenment. Happiness is the absence of loneliness. Well Adjusted is the absence of malice.

Spiritual Enlightenment is the means; to be happy and well adjusted is the end. This is the way of true evolution for all human beings.

THE FIVE EXCELLENCES

Spiritual Enlightenment results from mastering habits, this includes both thought habits and physical habits. To break these habits you must first bring awareness to your impulses, then consider their cause and effects, and finally decide whether to satisfy or replace them. The refinement of personal attributes is not a simple act of obeying a particular set of commandments; instead you must replace all commandments and hierarchies with a framework of the cosmos that is conducive to personal empowerment and individual spiritual enlightenment.

BREATHING

With the very first breath you took out of the womb, Chi entered your body in the form of air. With the very last breath that you take, Chi will leave your body in the form of air. A direct translation of the word Chi is breath, however, the exact same chinese character that is used to write the word "breath" is also used to write the word "blood" and the term "sex hormones," understanding this is essential for understanding why both sex and Tai Chi Chuan can be a Chi Kung exercise or ritual.

The purpose of Chi Kung exercises is to impose a disciplined, rhythmic pattern on your body movements and to condense the Chi within your breath, blood and sex organs.

Tai Chi Chuan is both a martial art and Chi Kung exercise. When performing Tai Chi Chuan your breath should be controlled by the natural expansion and contraction of your muscles. At the end of each breath there should be a natural pause this is called the point of retention. During the inhaled retention oxygen is absorbed by your lungs. During the exhaled retention your respiratory system rids itself of toxins and other waste.

Listen to the sound of your breath and cultivate an internal awareness of each phase flowing into the next, smoothly and without hindrance. When your breath is in motion your mind is in motion, by controlling your breath you can control your thoughts. At the inhaled retention point of every breath you take, the air divides into the essence of the five elements and nourishes your body with Chi, the intrinsic energy of the cosmos.

SLEEPING

Your external body uses sleep to rest and recuperate. Your internal body uses sleep to retune itself to the natural rhythms of nature and the cosmic emanations of Heaven and Earth. To relieve your body of the effects of the discordant emanations of daily stress you must create a transitional phase before actually going to bed. This may include stretching, bathing, meditating or many other appropriate activities.

Bringing awareness to the phases of sleep is the first step to mastering them. The complete sleep cycle consists of external consciousness, semi-consciousness, internal consciousness, and then back to semi-consciousness and external consciousness. In the twilight state of consciousness at both ends of the sleep cycle you can consciously enter the dream world and learn to master it.

Just as your physical body perceives an external world and can communicate this information to you, your sub-conscious mind perceives an internal world and can also communicate this information to you. When dreaming your sub-conscious mind is trying to convey a message directly to your conscious mind.

As you lay down to go to sleep resolve to enter the dream world and to remember as much as possible in the morning. While drifting through the state of semi-consciousness visualize stunning or erotic images. This will put what is normally an unconscious emotional response under control of the conscious mind. While in your dream state you should consciously change yourself into a tiger, a forest, practice shooting fire from your body and walk on the sun and the moon. You should also practice transforming things you see in your dream into different objects, an animal into man, water into fire, earth into space, one into many, many into one.

When you achieve a high level of ability in transforming dream images you can select the most significant image that gives the dream coherence and retain this image. This will enable you to awaken with full knowledge of the dream and comprehend its meaning. In the morning wake up slowly and bring as much of your dream world into consciousness as possible. Maintain the imagery of the dream without trying to analyze it, simply listen and learn.

By recording your dreams in a dream book you can watch their development over a period of time and evaluate the effects of your dreams on your life. This will help you maintain an unbroken continuity of consciousness throughout your waking and dream states; thus, cultivating deep insights into the nature of existence.

PROCREATING

The act of sexual intercourse creates an energy vortex of ecstasy that rises up through the internal centers of the two lovers and attracts down a spirit that already exist in the cosmic body. Once a spirit is attracted into the womb, a physical body is created as a temple to shelter the spirit in the natural world. Entering transcendental ecstasy through the doorway of sexual intercourse and natural herbs such as Hou Ma Ren, Ma Huang and Ling Chih has the power to take you beyond the natural world, to expand awareness, and to awaken sexual energy. In this condition you can reconnect your internal self with the spiritual realm. How do you recognize transcendental ecstasy? Sexual tension for both men and women usually builds up like a wound tension spring, and then at some point the tension is released and the spring unwinds producing useful energy. When ecstasy reaches a state of transcendence the tension in the spring is not released but is rather dissolved in the same way that water evaporates; therein showering down droplets of wisdom that dissolve social conventions and allow a spontaneous spiritual awareness. This is how the Tao is found and the illusion of separateness transcended.

EATING

The function of breath transformation is digestion; food descends to the stomach and is then transformed by the spleen at the interval between inhalation and exhalation. The transformed food separates into body waste and Chi, which mixes with the essence of water to produce blood. The function of your digestion works in concordance with the sun; early morning, midday, and early evenings are appropriate times for eating. At night you body works to a different rhythm and should not be burdened by excess food.

Your primary Tantien is the gastric fire of digestion, your lower abdomen, is the cauldron that contains that fire. When you fan the flames of your lower abdomen your Chi burns up all of the impurities of the body, confusions of the mind, and spiritual obstacles of life.

During the year, the eight dates of the solstices, equinoxes and beginnings are celebrated with a twenty-four fast. One method of cleaning out your internal organs and systems is to eliminate a succession of products from your diet over a period of three to ten days, then drink only fresh squeezed juices and herbal teas for a period of one to three days. Add food back to your diet consciously and with discrimination. Starting with fresh fruits, vegetables and whole unprocessed foods, consider which items you truly want, instead of feeling imposed on or denied.

A true fast consists of nothing but water; the body absorbs no nutrition of any kind. Fasting and prolonged exposure to the natural elements can awaken a sense of detachment, concentrate the mind, purify the emotions and cultivate a relationship between your internal body and the cosmos.

WORKING

As long as you dwell in the natural world you must consider the practical aspects of life. You cannot be indifferent to the suffering of others yet, you must live and work in the world and not let it effect you. Thrive but do not embrace unhealthy prosperity. Take time to observe the beauty around you so that you may survive and grow even through the struggles of life. You must not spend all of your time and energy to accumulate more that you can use but rather, develop skills that can be used as a method of supporting yourself as well as helping others find dignity and meaning in life.

To live a natural and simple life does not require poverty or self-denial, it requires simplicity in everything you do. When you make a natural and simple life your way of living and it will affect changes in your mind, body and spirit.

The cosmic vibration of our original source has existed since the beginning of the time, yet only those who are in harmony with it can hear it. Listen for the sound of the true Tao and you will hear the cosmic vibration. What is the source of human knowledge? The Tao. What is the nature of human knowledge? Yin and Yang. This is the Scripture of the Tao, it neglects no one, and can be denied to no one.

Living in retirement beyond the world,
Silently enjoying isolation,
I pull the rope of my door tighter
and bind firmly this cracked window.
My spirit is tuned to the Spring season
At the fall of the year there is autumn in my heart.
Thus, imitating cosmic changes
My cottage becomes a Universe.

LU YUN (Fourth Century A.D.)

SHADOWBOOK

Appendix

SHADOWBOOK

pithy verses that lead to unfoldment
just as the pith of a flower leads to
the unfoldment of its petals

FASTING

Spring Cleansing Cocktail
One pinch of Cayenne Pepper
Two tablespoons of Lemon Juice
Two tablespoons of Maple Syrup
Eight ounces of Spring Water

Short Cleanse
Eliminate
Meat and dairy foods
Nuts, seeds and grains

Drink only fruit juices,
A light vegetable broth and the
Spring Cleansing Cocktail

Eat salads and fresh fruits
Add, nuts seeds and grains
Then, meats and dairy foods

And, finally consider which
Items you wish to add

Without feeling imposed on
Or denied

Moderate Cleanse
Eliminate
Meat and fish
Then, dairy foods
Then, nuts, seeds, and grains

Drink lots of water
Fruit juices and Herb Teas

Drink only fruit juices
And, the Spring Cleansing Cocktail

Eat salads and fruit
A clear vegetable broth for dinner

Add, nuts seeds and grains
Then, dairy foods
Then, meat and fish

And, finally consider which
Items you wish to add
Without feeling imposed on
Or denied

Long Cleanse
Eliminate
Meat
Then, fish
Dairy foods
Nuts, seeds
And, grains

Eat fruit and vegetables
And, drink only Herb Teas

Eat fruit and drink only
Fruit juices and Herb Teas

Drink only the Spring
Cleansing Cocktail and
Herb Teas for three days

Add, fruit
Then, salad and
A clear vegetable broth
For dinner

Then, nuts and seeds
Grains and dairy foods
Fish and meat

MEDITATING

Immortal Spirit
Close your Eyes and sit;
    As if you are a
"Stone Pillar supporting
    Heaven and Earth"

Let Thoughts and
    Emotions pass by
"Out of silence, rises up
    Immortal Spirit "

Shang Tantien
Place a Candleflame
    At eye level,

In a darkened room
    About three feet away

"Look with fixed eyes;
    'til tears are shed"

Then, while keeping your
    Inner Gaze steady;
Close your eyes
    And bring the image
Of the candleflame
    To your Shang Tantien

Cosmic Sphere
Sit cross-legged in
    The center of
A cosmic sphere

"Neither the past;
    Nor the future exist "

What is divided by
    The forces of nature,
Can be united by the
    The spirit of man

DAWN

Nourishing The Breath
Early in the Morning;
    Stand up with Chest
    thrown out
And Abdomen drawn in
    While slowly inhaling

Then, hold your breath
  As you snappily
Slap the Qihai, Guanyuan
  And Zhongji points
  with one palm
And pat the Mingmen point
  With the other palm

Finally, rub the palms together
  Until they are warm,
Then use one palm to rub
the Mingmen point
  and the other
Palm to rub the Qihai,
  Guanyuan

And Zhongji points

DUSK

Nourshing The Kidneys
Before going to bed
  Sit cross-legged
With eyes closed and
  Bring awareness to your breath

Supporting the Hui Yin
  With one palm,
Massage the Qihai,
  Guanyuan and Zhongji Points
With the other palm
  Until you feel a warm sensation Spreading over the Tantien

Three Breaths
Rapid breathing is incompatible
    with calm
And, tends to scatter the thoughts

Panting is irregular and gives rise
    to coughing which is
Known as Rebellion of the Breath

Heavy breathing without being
    noisy demands
An effort that produces fatigue

Breathing that is Attenuated
    Condensed and Imperceptible
"Opens the door to the natural
    emanations of Heaven and Earth "

Four Brocades
Mountain Pose
Lift palms to shoulder level
Facing downward
One palm in front and
One palm in back
Inhale lift and hold breath
Exhale lower palms and
Return to Mountain

Mountain pose
Lift arms forward with
Palms down to shoulder level
Open arms to sides with
Palm edge down and
Return to Mountain

Mountain pose
Bend arms at waist level
Rotate shoulders
Inhale shrugging up
Exhale sinking down
In two directions
Return to Mountain

Mountain pose
Inhale and create
Tension like drawing
Apowerful bow
Exhale and release tension
Like shooting an arrow

Five Animals Chi Kung

Tiger
Take a deep breath
Clench and raise Claws
As if hoisting a heavy load
While swallowing air
For thirty-two repetitions

Bear
Take a deep breath
Clench and raise both Paws
Looking left and right
Alternate paws reaching
For the sky

Stag
Take a deep breath
Clench and raise both Antlers

Lower your head slightly
And direct your mind
To your lower back

Monkey
Take a deep breath
Stand on one foot and
Clasp the trunk of a tree
With the other arm

Swallow air
While plucking fruit
Until you perspire

Crane
Take a deep breath
Lift and spread Wings
With one on top of other

Looking upward
Lengthen the spine and
Imagine that you are ready to fly

Six Reunions
The Oneness of
Mind and Body
Is cultivated through
The Six Reunions

Three of the reunions are
Shoulders and Ribs
Elbows and Knees
Knees and Feet

Three of the reunions are
Intent and Knowledge
Knowledge and Breath
Breath and Strength

Where the rules of posture
And conduct are not
Properly followed disruption

And disorder will result

Seven Remedies

Anger
Stroke the Taichong
With pad of middle finger
And, rub the Shanzhong,
Qihai and Neiguan points
With the pads of your thumbs

Close your eyes and place
The tip of your tongue
On the Palate
Breath in deeply with the nose
And, out quickly with mouth

Grief and Melancholy
Stroke the Ermen, Qingming
And, Yingxiang points
With your middle fingers
While rubbing the Renzhong point
With your thumb

Close your eyes and place
The tip of your tongue
On the palate
Inhale slowly with the nose
And, exhale with your mouth

Move both hands in circles
Massaging the abdomen and ribs
Stroke the Shanzhong,
Juque, Shangwan, Zhongwan,
Xiawan and Quhai points

Fear and Terror
Use your thumbs to rub the
Daling, Shenmen, Taiyang
And, Yangchi points

Close your eyes
And, place the tip of your tongue
On the palate

Breath in deeply
With your nose
And, out slowly
With your mouth

Rub the Guanyuan
With the left palm
And, the Mingmen
With the right palm
For three minutes

Joy
Sit cross-legged

With eyes closed
While breathing slowly
For five to ten minutes

With eyes still closed
Use your thumbs to
to press and rub the
Daling and Sanyinjiao
Points

Anxiety
Sit cross-legged
With eyes closed
While breathing slowly
For fifteen minutes

With eyes still closed
Press and rub the
Xuehai with middle fingers

With one palm placed
Above another
Press and rub the
Guanyuan point

With the fingertips of
Both hands pointed toward
Each other stroke the
Yintang, Shenting, Baihui
And Fengfu points

With the four fingers of
Each hand drawn together
Press and rub the nape
Of your neck

These methods will
Circulate the Blood
Tranquilize the Mind
And, supplement your Chi

Eighty-eight Forms
Heaven and Earth
Wild Horses Shear the Mane
Tide Washes In and Out
The Crane
Rest on High Mountain
White Crane Spreads Its Wings
Part the North Wind
Play the Pei Pah
Part the North Wind
Play the Pei Pah
Rams Head Punch
Dragon Flame
Embrace Tiger & Return to Mountain

Tide Washes In and Out
The Crane
Rams Head Punch
Receding Waves
Diagonal Flying
Rest on High Mountain
White Crane Spreads its Wings
Part the North Wind
Take the Blossom
Reaping Wind
Pounding Wave
Whipping Branch
Rams Head Punch
Tide Washes In and Out

The Crane
Open and Close Wings
The Crane

High Pat on Horse
Lightening Kick
Dragon Stamp
Part the South Wind
Rams Head Punch
Dart Tongue
Spit Poisen
Whipping Branch
Rams Head Punch
Dragon Stamp
Ride the Tiger
Lightening Kick
Twin Dragons Seek Out the Moon
Lightening Kick
Dragon Stamp
Whipping Branch
Rams Head Punch
Dragon Flame
Embrace Tiger & Return to Mountain

Tide Washes In and Out
The Crane
Wild Horse Shears Its Mane
Tide washes In and Out
The Crane
Dark Lady Spins Flax
Tide Washes In and Out
The Crane
Open and Close Wings
The Crane

Cobra Descends
The Stork
Receding Waves
Diagonal Flying
Rest on High Mountain
White Crane Spreads its Wings
Part the North Wind
Pluck Flower
Reaping Wind
Pounding Wave
Whipping Branch
Tide Washes In and Out
The Crane
Open and Close Wings
The Crane
High Pat on Horse
Cobra Spits Poisen
Dragon Stamp
Rams Head Punch
Tide Washes In and Out
The Crane
Cobra Descends
Seven Stars
Cobra Spits Poisen
Lotus Kick
Ride the Tiger
Rams Head Punch
Dragon Flame
Embrace Tiger & Return to Mountain

Afterword

"Who the Hell are you? And, where the Hell did you get this information? I've been in the business for twenty years and I've never read anything like this!"

These are the words that greeted me when I called Marvin Smalheiser the editor of T'AI CHI magazine in regards to an article I had submitted for publication, entitled "Application of the 13 techniques and San Shou."

After explaining that I got my information from studying with David Wu Ph.D. of the university of MN. who is the only man ever to receive a Doctorate with a Dissertation written on the subject of Tai Chi Chuan, Mr. Smalheiser agreed to publish the article but only if I got permission from David to attach my name to his reputation. Permission was granted and the article was published in October of 1993.

I have expanded the article into "Tao of Heaven." The core of this book is a biomechanical description of the Thirteen Forms of Tai Chi Chuan that is unlike and more complete than any other description of its kind. All other books on the subject incorrectly describe the Thirteen Forms of Tai Chi Chuan as being comprised of either; "Five Hand shapes and Eight Stances" or the "Original 13" striking, kicking, and blocking techniques.

Only in cryptic documents handed down from ancient times and David Wu's Dissertation is the true essence of the Thirteen Forms revealed. That true essence is this; each of the Thirteen Forms represents a function rather than a specific technique.

Notes

Introduction

The Three Orders referred to in the ancient poem are Heaven, Earth, and Man. Man is considered the second of the Three orders because he exists in between Heaven and Earth.

Fu- His, is the legendary emperor and creator of the I-Ching. Shen Nung, is the legendary emperor and creator of agriculture and Ancient Chinese Herbology. Huang Ti, is the legendary emperor and creator of Ancient Chinese medicine and rituals.

Peng, is one of the Eight Great Immortals who visited Sloppy Chang and taught him Tai Chi Chuan.

Chapter One

This Ancient Chinese version of "genesis" grew out of a shamanistic culture and is completely substantiated by western science. Indeed, this framework of the cosmos is the original Big Bang theory and the foundation of modern physics, out of nothingness came a single particle, which fragmented and multiplied to produce everything that exist.

The analogy of the balloon with dots on it representing the expansion of the cosmos was first made be Sir A.S. Eddington in 1930.

Chapter Two

This chapter begins anew with the Ancient Chinese theory of physics and how they are applied to human anatomy and physiology.

Ancient Chinese drawings of the sexual postures of the Eight Methods of Therapy can be found in many sources including,"Sexual

Secrets, The Alchemy of Ecstasy," by Nik Douglas & Penny Slinger and also "Secret Sexual Positions," by Kenneth Ray Stubbs Ph.D.

Chapter Three

This is the core chapter of the book and is based on my training and experience with David Wu Ph.D. The chapter begins with an ancient and well-accepted description of the Thirteen Forms and reproach from the mystical master that both the substance and function of the Thirteen Forms must be clearly discriminated in the practice of Tai Chi Chuan.

Chapter Four

This chapter expands on the biomechanical description of the Thirteen Forms by clearly explaining and demonstrating their practical application in more advanced training drills in which opponents are actually attacking and defending.

Chapter Five

Again, this chapter expands on the biomechanical description of the Thirteen Forms by explaining their relationship to solo-sequence training or Shadowboxing.

Chapter Six

The Five Excellences of Breathing, Sleeping, Procreating, Eating, and Working, presented in this section are provided for informational purposes only. If you suspect you may have a medical problem seek out a professional before beginning any treatment.

The three herbs listed in the section on procreation are Hou Ma Ren (marijuana), Ma Huang (ephedra), and Ling Chih (psilocybin mushrooms).

Bibliography

The development of Tai Chi Chuan was deeply influenced by doctrine and literature that can be traced back over 3,000 years. There are records of breathing exercises in the Jin Wen (writings on bronzes) of the Zhou dynasty (1100-221 B.C.). On one cultural relic of the Warring States Period (770-221 B.C.) the following words were engraved: "Take a deep breath and sink it to the tantian. Hold the breath there for a while and then exhale it like the sprouting of grass until it goes to the top of your head. In this way, the yang energy will go up and yin will go down. Those who yang or yin energy goes its own way will live, otherwise they will die."

In Changsha, the capital of Hunan Province, a number of medical treatises and books on breathing exercises from the Western Han dynasty (206 B.C.-24 A.D.) were discovered at an excavation site, including forty-four pieces of silk with painted figures of men and women of all ages doing various movements combined with breathing, the words "look skyward and exhale" were inscribed beside one figure. Some of the movements imitated the Tiger, Stag, Bear, Crane, and Monkey, which later became Wuqinxi or Five Animals of Chi Kung.

The first recorded article that directly related the Taoist doctrine to both push-hands and the Tai Chi Chuan solo sequence was "Tai Chi Chuan Lun" by Wang Tsung-yueh (1736-1795 A.D.) Wang Tsung-yueh also wrote the "Song of Push-hands" and the Thirteen Postures and Long Chuan. In these documents, Look Left, Look Right, Advance, Retreat, and Central Equilibrium are clearly established as the Five elements; while Push, Rollback, Ward-off, Press, Elbow stroke, Split,

Pluck and Shoulder stroke are clearly established as the Eight Trigrams. Thus, making the Five Elements and the Eight Trigrams the Thirteen Forms of Tai Chi Chuan.

Bian, Zhong. "Qigong: Its origin and Development" (1990). Martial Arts of China, published monthly by China Direct Publishing Inc., San Francisco CA.

Blofeld, John. "I Ching" (1968). E.P. Dutton & Co., Inc.

Chao, H.C. "The Secrets of Shaolin Internal Kung Fu" (1985). Meadea Enterprises Co., Inc. Republic of China.

Chao, H.C. "The Unseen Mind Force of Kung Fu" (1986). Meadea Enterprises Co., Inc. Republic of China.

Cheng, Man-Ch'ing. "Cheng Tzu's Thirteen Treatises on T'ai Chi Ch'uan" (1985). Translated by Benjamin Pang Jeng Lo and Martin Inn. North Atlanic Books, Berkeley, California.

Deshimaru, Taisen. "The Zen Way to the Martial Arts" (1982). I.P. Dutton, New York.

Douglas,Nik and Slinger,Penny. "Sexual Secrets-the Alchemy of Ecstasy" (1979). Destiny Books, Rochester, Vermont.

Duke, Mark. "Acupuncture" (1973). A Pyramid Book by Pyramid Communications, Inc.

Fazzioli, Eduardo. "Chinese Calligraphy, from Pictograph to Ideogram: The History of 214 Essential Chinese/Japanese Characters" (1987). Abbeville Publishing Group, New York, New York.

Ferris, Timothy. "The Creation of the Universe" (1985). Northstar Associates, Boston.

Hyatt, Richard. "Chinese Herbal Medicine, Ancient Art and Modern Science" with Therapeutic Repertory by Feldman, Robert, M.D. (1987). Schocken Books, New York.

Liang, T.T., Master. "Tai Chi Ch'uan for Health and Self Defense" (1977). Vintage Books, a division of Random House, Inc.

McClure, Vimala. "The Ethics of Love, Using Yoga's Timeless Wisdom to Heal Yourself, Others, and the Earth" (1992). NUCLEUS Publications, Willow Springs, MO.

Mianyu, Qu. "Taijiquan-A Medical Assessment," Martial Arts of China (Volume 1, No. 5, 1990).

Ni, Hua-Ching, The Later Teachings of Lao Tzu" (1995). Shambhala Publications, Inc.

Porkert, Manfred M.D. with Dr. Christian Ullmann. "Chinese Medicine" (1982). Translated and adapted by Mark Howson. William Morrow and Company, Inc.

Sherman, W. Irwin and Sherman, G. Vilia. "Biology-A Human Approach" (1983). Oxford University Press, New York.

Veith, Ilza. "The Yellow Emperor's Classic of Internal Medicine" (1949). University of California Press, New edition 1972

Wieger, L., S.H., Dr. "Chinese Characters, Their Origin, Etymology, History, Classification and Signification. A Thorough study from Chinese Documents" (1965). This edition is also a joint publication of Paragon Book Reprint Corp. and Dover Publication, Inc. The first edition of Chinese Characters was published in 1915.

Wing, R. L. "The I Ching Workbook" (1979). Bantam Doubleday Dell Publishing Group, Inc.

Wu, David J. Ph.D. "The Biomechanical Analysis of the Tai Chi fixed-Step, Single Push-Hand Movement." A PhD. Dissertation submitted to the faculty of the Graduate School of the University of Minnesota in 1990. Degree granted March 1991.

Zhiquang, Feng and Dabiao, Feng. "Chen Style Taijiquan" (1948). Compiled by Zhaohua Publishing House, Beijing, China and published by Hai Feng Publishing co, Hong Kong, China.

Index

About the Author

Sifu keven-san is a scholar of Ancient Chinese Medicine, Art and Philosophy. He is an extraordinary teacher who has taught hundreds of people to clearly discriminate both the substance and function of the Thirteen Forms in terms so simple that students can memorize them verbatim and apply them with a degree of effectiveness in a single lesson.